FACING
HOMOPHOBIA

Other Books in the LIVING PROUD! Series

FACING HOMOPHOBIA

Robert Rodi and Laura Ross

Foreword by Kevin Jennings
Founder, GLSEN (the Gay, Lesbian & Straight
Education Network)

MASON CREST

Mason Crest
450 Parkway Drive, Suite D
Broomall, PA 19008
www.masoncrest.com

Printed in the United States of America

First printing
9 8 7 6 5 4 3 2 1

Series ISBN: 978-1-4222-3501-0
Hardcover ISBN: 978-1-4222-3508-9
ebook ISBN: 978-1-4222-8381-3

Cataloging-in-Publication Data is available on file at the Library of Congress.

Developed and Produced by Print Matters Productions, Inc. (www.printmattersinc.com)
Cover and Interior Design by Kris Tobiassen, Matchbook Digital

Picture credits: 10, Matthew Shepard Foundation; 12, Jed Conklin/ZUMA Press/Newscom; 16, Matthew Shepard Foundation; 17, Cane/Gabay Productions/Good Machine/Home Box Office/Album/ Newscom; 22, Jeff Malet Photography/Newscom; 25, AJ Alfieri-Crispin; 27, Zurich Central Library/ Wikimedia Creative Commons; 29, Rama/Wikimedia Creative Commons; 32, Jason Lawrence/ JLaw45/Wikimedia Creative Commons; 32, Jason Lawrence/JLaw45/Wikimedia Creative Commons; 34, Patsy Lynch/Polaris/Newscom; 38, Kevin Dooley/kevindooley/Wikimedia Creative Commons; 39, Randy Stern/resedabear/Wikimedia Creative Commons; 41, Wikimedia Creative Commons; 43, dbking; 46, Mike Theiler/EPA/Newscom; 48, Jackie Alexander/jackealexander/Wikimedia Creative Commons; 51, Fiskot/Wikimedia Creative Commons; 53, istolethetv/Wikimedia Creative Commons **Front cover:** Syda Productions/Shutterstock

FACING
HOMOPHOBIA

CONTENTS

KEY ICONS TO LOOK FOR

 Text-Dependent Questions: These questions send the reader back to the text for more careful attention to the evidence presented there.

 Words to Understand: These words with their easy-to-understand definitions will increase the reader's understanding of the text while building vocabulary skills.

 Series Glossary of Key Terms: This back of the book glossary contains terminology used throughout this series. Words found here increase the reader's ability to read and comprehend higher-level books and articles in this field.

 Research Projects: Readers are pointed toward areas of further inquiry connected to each chapter. Suggestions are provided for projects that encourage deeper research and analysis.

 Sidebars: This boxed material within the main text allows readers to build knowledge, gain insights, explore possibilities, and broaden their perspectives by weaving together additional information to provide realistic and holistic perspectives.

FOREWORD

I loved libraries as a kid.

Every Saturday my mom and I would drive from the trailer where we lived on an unpaved road in the unincorporated town of Lewisville, North Carolina, and make the long drive to the "big city" of Winston-Salem to go to the downtown public library, where I would spend joyous hours perusing the books on the shelves. I'd end up lugging home as many books as my arms could carry and generally would devour them over the next seven days, all the while eagerly anticipating next week's trip. The library opened up all kinds of worlds to me—all kinds of worlds, except a gay one.

Oh, I found some "gay" books, even in the dark days of the 1970s. I'm not sure how I did, but I found my way to authors like Tennessee Williams, Yukio Mishima, and Gore Vidal. While these great artists created masterpieces of literature that affirmed that there were indeed other gay people in the universe, their portrayals of often-doomed gay men hardly made me feel hopeful about my future. It was better than nothing, but not much better. I felt so lonely and isolated I attempted to take my own life my junior year of high school.

In the 35 years since I graduated from high school in 1981, much has changed. Gay–straight alliances (an idea my students and I pioneered at Concord Academy in 1988) are now widespread in American schools. Out LGBT (lesbian, gay, bisexual, and transgender) celebrities and programs with LGBT themes are commonplace on the airwaves. Oregon has a proud bisexual governor, multiple members of Congress are out as lesbian, gay, or bisexual, and the White House was bathed in rainbow colors the day marriage equality became the law of the land in 2015. It gets better, indeed.

So why do we need the Living Proud! series?

- Because GLSEN (the Gay, Lesbian & Straight Education Network) reports that over two-thirds of LGBT students routinely hear anti-LGBT language at school

- Because GLSEN reports that over 60% of LGBT students do not feel safe at school
- Because the CDC (the Centers for Disease Control and Prevention, a U.S. government agency) reports that lesbian and gay students are four times more likely to attempt suicide than heterosexual students

In my current role as the executive director of the Arcus Foundation (the world's largest financial supporter of LGBT rights), I work in dozens of countries and see how far there still is to go. In over 70 countries same-sex relations are crimes under existing laws: in 8, they are a crime punishable by the death penalty. It's better, but it's not all better—especially in our libraries, where there remains a need for books that address LGBT issues that are appropriate for young people, books that will erase both the sense of isolation so many young LGBT people still feel as well as the ignorance so many non-LGBT young people have, ignorance that leads to the hate and violence that still plagues our community, both at home and abroad.

The Living Proud! series will change that and will save lives. By providing accurate, age-appropriate information to young people of all sexual orientations and gender identities, the Living Proud! series will help young people understand the complexities of the LGBT experience. Young LGBT people will see themselves in its pages, and that reflection will help them see a future full of hope and promise. I wish Living Proud! had been on the shelves of the Winston-Salem/Forsyth County Public Library back in the seventies. It would have changed my life. I'm confident that it will have as big an impact on its readers today as it would have had on me back then. And I commend it to readers of any age.

Kevin Jennings
Founder, GLSEN (the Gay, Lesbian & Straight Education Network)
Executive Director, Arcus Foundation

GLSEN®

GLSEN is the leading national education organization focused on ensuring safe and affirming schools for all students. GLSEN seeks to develop school climates where difference is valued for the positive contribution it makes to creating a more vibrant and diverse community. www.glsen.org

The spirit of Matthew Shepard (1976–1998) lives on in the Matthew Shepard and James Byrd, Jr. Hate Crimes Prevention Act, which was signed into law in 2009.

1
WHAT'S SO SCARY ABOUT DIFFERENCE?

 WORDS TO UNDERSTAND

Hate crime: An illegal act in which the victim is targeted because of his or her race, religion, sexual orientation, gender, gender identity, disability, ethnicity, or other identity characteristic.

Homophobia: The fear and hatred of homosexuality. A homophobic person is sometimes referred to as a "homophobe."

Civil rights: The rights of a citizen to personal and political freedom under the law.

Discrimination: Unfair treatment of a group based on prejudice against them.

On the night of October 6, 1998, a University of Wyoming freshman, Matthew Shepard, was approached by Aaron McKinney and Russell Henderson at the Fireside Lounge in Laramie, Wyoming. The three young men talked and had a few drinks, and at the end of the night, McKinney and Henderson offered Matthew a ride home. But the ride took an ugly turn. Matthew was robbed, beaten, and tortured, then tied to a fence in a remote area overlooking the lights of Laramie. Having found his address in his wallet, McKinney and Henderson left him to die, planning to burglarize his apartment.

Eighteen hours later, a cyclist, Aaron Kriefels, came across what he thought was a beat-up old scarecrow. It turned out to be Matthew, still lashed to the fence, in a coma, and near death. He had fractures to his skull and severe brain stem damage. He was rushed to the intensive care

An artist placed seven effigies on fences around Jackson Hole, Wyoming to commemorate the fifth anniversary of Matthew Shepard's murder.

unit at Poudre Valley Hospital in Fort Collins, Colorado, where he was placed on full life support. The medical staff determined that his injuries were too severe for treatment. Matthew never regained consciousness and was pronounced dead at 12:53 a.m. on October 12, 1998. He was twenty-one years old.

A Tragic Symbol of Homophobia

Matthew Shepard was the son of Dennis and Judy Shepard; he had a younger brother named Logan. Matthew was a bright young man studying political science and was chosen as the student representative for the Wyoming Environmental Council. He had many friends and a close extended family. His father described him as "an optimistic and accepting young man who had a special gift of relating to almost everyone. He was the type of person who was very approachable and always looked to new challenges." Matthew was also a gay man, well known in his college community for his openness and, as his father said, for his "great passion for equality and . . . for the acceptance of people's differences."

Matthew's murder was quickly identified by the media and members of the Laramie LGBT community and their allies as a **hate crime**. Aaron McKinney and Russell Henderson were arrested and tried for the crime. At the trial, Chasity Pasley and Kristen Price, girlfriends of McKinney and Henderson, proved key witnesses. In a statement, Price told authorities that McKinney had revealed to her that he and

Henderson went to the bar bathroom and made a plan to pretend to be gay so as to get Shepard into the truck to rob him.

McKinney and Henderson never denied that they'd committed the crime. McKinney pleaded the "gay panic defense," claiming that he was so terrified by Matthew's supposed sexual advances toward him that he was driven to temporary insanity. Henderson pleaded guilty without a trial. Their lawyers argued that because of the "gay panic defense" the two men were not responsible for their actions.

Both McKinney and Henderson were found guilty of felony murder, making them eligible for the death penalty in Wyoming. What happened next surprised some. Matthew Shepard's father made an emotional statement in the courtroom, asking that, in memory of his murdered son's compassion, the judge sentence the killers to life imprisonment rather than impose the ultimate punishment of death.

Tragically, the hate that caused Matthew's death haunted his funeral at St. Mark's Episcopal Church on October 16, 1998. Across the street from the church, members of the conservative-fringe Westboro Baptist Church carried signs that read "GOD HATES FAGS" and "MATT SHEPARD ROTS IN HELL."

Anti-gay Hate Crimes

The death of Matthew Shepard and the trial of the young men who so brutally murdered him brought the issue of **homophobia** and its tragic consequences to the attention of the American people, as the media closely covered the story. This promising young man became a symbol for the many less-well-known victims of homophobia in its many forms. But almost two decades later, the number of hate crimes against LGBT people continues to rise. According to FBI statistics, there were more than 1,400 such crimes reported in 2014—but estimates for the actual number of violent crimes against people identified as LGBT are much higher. Since many states do not legally recognize "anti-LGBT hate crimes" as a category, and many LGBT people are, for various reasons, afraid to report them.

The LGBT community and its allies have been demanding—and slowly gaining—full legal and **civil rights**. Their opponents on the religious and political right, however, have been stepping up their own organized efforts *against* LGBT rights, summoning up the same homophobic language and arguments that have been used to oppress gay people for centuries.

Why, in the 21st century, are LGBT people still being denied the rights to housing, employment, and job security that are guaranteed to their fellow citizens? Why are they still in danger of being harassed, beaten, and even killed on the streets of American cities? Why are they still being condemned from the pulpits of churches and by conservative talk show hosts? Why are they still being bullied in the hallways of America's schools, and mocked and stereotyped in the media? Progress is being made, but homophobia is still very much alive in our world.

Judy Shepard, Matthew Shepard's mother, together with her husband Dennis, founded the Matthew Shepard Foundation to encourage understanding of and equality for LGBT people.

CLOSE-UP: THE MATTHEW SHEPARD FOUNDATION

In an attempt to turn tragedy and hate into love and hope, Matthew Shepard's mother, Judy Shepard, started a foundation in her late son's name, whose longstanding mission is "to erase hate by replacing it with understanding, compassion and acceptance. Through local, regional and national outreach, we empower individuals to find their voice to create change and challenge communities to identify and address hate that lives within their schools, neighborhoods and homes."

Among the Foundation's success stories are its role in passing the federal Matthew Shepard and James Byrd, Jr. Hate Crimes Prevention Act; nearly 1,000 public speaking engagements promoting acceptance of diversity; support for hundreds of productions of *The Laramie Project*, a play created by Moisés Kaufman and members of the Tectonic Theater Project about the range of reactions to Matthew's murder; and "Matthew's Place," an online support community for teens and young adults.

Gay award-winning writer-director-producer Moisés Kaufman, shown here, created *The Laramie Project* with members of the Tectonic Theater Project. The play was based on hundreds of interviews with people from Laramie, Wyoming, about how their lives and their town had been affected by the murder of Matthew Shepard. It was produced as an HBO movie in 2002.

Fear of the Other

Imagine that it's 40,000 years ago, on the bitter-cold tundra of what is now southwestern France. A group of hungry hunters are tracking a wounded wooly mammoth, an extinct ancestor of the elephant. These hunters are humans, but not quite like us. They are stockier, stronger, and—by our standards—a lot uglier. They are Neanderthals.

Meanwhile, another group of hunters, taller and slimmer and looking more or less like us (Cro-Magnons) are about to cross paths with the bulky Neanderthals. What's going to happen when they meet?

Some archaeologists have theorized that the Cro-Magnons, modern humans who had evolved in Africa, killed off the Neanderthals as they moved into their European homeland. They cite it as an ancient example of genocide, the murder of an entire people because they are different. The Cro-Magnons didn't like the way the Neanderthals looked, and they didn't want to share their hunting grounds with them. The Neanderthals were "the Other," and they became extinct through their contact with modern humans.

There seems to be something deep in the most primitive part of our brain that dislikes, distrusts, and fears those who look or dress or pray or act differently from ourselves. Time and again throughout human history, encounters with the Other turned hostile and violent. People in one valley hated the people in the next valley for no reason except that they always had. Tribes fought other tribes. Nations fought other nations. Neighboring countries created nasty stereotypes about each other.

As people began to explore the world, they came in contact with one another as never before—but they carried their fear of the Other with them. The story of the colonization of North and South America and Africa is riddled with racism, slavery, and genocide. While saints and philosophers throughout the ages have tried to help us see the grave error of hating, fearing, or mistrusting our fellow human beings just because they are different, progress toward mutual respect and understanding has been painfully slow.

On a smaller scale, within families and communities, that same primitive part of our brain has long been a factor in how we relate to the Other. People who are different from the majority in any way have faced **discrimination**, fear, and rejection. Religions have tended to present what is most common as sacred and what might be uncommon as evil, while society's laws and customs have rewarded the majority and punished the minority.

 CLOSE-UP: PREJUDICED PEOPLE AREN'T PICKY

Sociologists have found that people who are prejudiced toward one group of people also tend to be prejudiced toward other groups. In a study done in 1946, people were asked about their attitudes concerning a variety of ethnic groups, including Danireans, Pirraneans, and Wallonians. The study found that people who were prejudiced toward blacks and Jews also distrusted these other three groups.

The catch is that Danireans, Pirraneans, and Wallonians don't exist! The researchers made them up just to see whether people would hate others they'd never even heard of—and they did! Clearly, prejudice is in the mind of the person and not based on any real differences in groups that might inspire it.

Prejudice

The root word of *prejudice* is *pre-judge*. Prejudiced people judge others based purely on the fact that they *are* "other"—because they belong to a different group. They make assumptions about others that have no basis in reality. They believe that if a person's skin is a different shade, if he speaks a different language, wears different clothes, or worships God in a different way—or falls in love in a different way—then he is somehow unworthy. The prejudiced person believes that this other person is not as smart, nice, honest, valuable, or moral as he himself is. In fact, he's pretty sure that the person is stupid, inferior, dishonest, and downright BAD.

Why do human beings have these feelings? Sociologists believe that we have a basic tendency to fear anything that's unfamiliar or unknown. Ever since the Cro-Magnons ran into the Neanderthals, we have been assuming that if someone is strange (not like us), then that person is also scary; he's automatically a threat to us.

If we allow ourselves get to know the strangers, of course, we end up discovering that they're not so different from ourselves; they're not so frightening and threatening after all. But too often, we don't let that happen. We put up a wall between ourselves and the strangers. We're on the inside; they're on the outside. Then we peer over the wall, too far away from the others to see anything but how different they are.

The idea of "the Other" continues to support racism, sexism, homophobia, transphobia and prejudice of all kinds. It holds us back from the progress we need to make as human beings on this planet. Stereotypes, misunderstandings, and ignorance have kept us from being able to appreciate that if we learn to honor our diversity—our unique individual qualities—then we strengthen our communities and support the health and safety of our Earth. We need to try to get beyond that primitive part of our brain that fears and rejects those who might be different and get to know one another better. That may be the only way we'll ever get past prejudice.

 TEXT-DEPENDENT QUESTIONS

- Why was Matthew Shepard's murder called a "hate crime"?
- Why is the number of anti-gay hate crimes recorded in any given year likely not to reflect how many actually occurred?
- What do sociologists say is the cause of prejudice?

 RESEARCH PROJECTS

- Search out your own state's policies regarding hate crimes; see if LGBT people are included.
- Make a list of the ways homophobia and transphobia are like racial or religious prejudice, and the ways in which they're different.
- Visit the Matthew Shepard Foundation website and check out its latest projects and programs.

Gay rights activists at the Lincoln Memorial in Washington, D.C.

2

HOMOPHOBIA AND ITS VICTIMS

 WORDS TO UNDERSTAND

Sexual orientation: A person's physical and emotional attraction to males, females, or both.
Heretics: People who disagree with the religious establishment; in the past, they were often punished for their beliefs.
Sodomy: Any human sexual act that is not oriented toward reproduction (though the term has often been used specifically for homosexual behavior).
Liberal: Refers to new ideas that support social change.
Persecuted: Mistreated and oppressed.
Stigma: A mark of shame.

Homophobia is a particular kind of prejudice. It's the fear of the Other when that other person's sexual behaviors are different from your own. The suffix "phobia" refers to feelings of intense fear and hatred—so "homo" + "phobia" means fear and hatred of homosexuals.

How Common Is Homosexuality?

Estimates vary as to the number of LGBT people in the population because significant numbers of people don't want to identify themselves as LGBT to a pollster. A 2014 Centers for Disease Control survey found 1.6% of adults over 18 identified as gay or lesbian, 0.7% identified as bisexual, and 1.1% didn't know or declined to answer. A 2011 survey came up with a higher percentage with an estimated 3.5% of adults identifying as lesbian, gay, or bisexual and 0.3% as transgender. We may never know the exact numbers, but we do know that there are literally millions of our fellow citizens who are being stereotyped, discriminated against, denied their full civil rights, and even threatened with violent crimes simply because of their **sexual orientation**—simply because they are gay, lesbian, bisexual, or transgender.

Right now, homophobia is negatively affecting the lives of millions of people—people in your community, people you know, people you care about, maybe even you. LGBT people are everywhere, and, unfortunately, so are homophobes.

While some homophobic people call homosexuality a "crime against nature," nature seems to feel differently. Scientists have discovered that same-sex sexual behavior is very common in the animal kingdom: It has been observed in close to 1,500 species and is well-documented in over five hundred, including black swans, mallard ducks, penguins, apes, elephants, giraffes, sheep, hyenas, lizards, and even fruit flies! Same-sex penguin pairs mate for life and sometimes even raise orphaned chicks together. According to researcher Petter Bøckman, "No species has been found in which homosexual behavior has *not* been shown to exist, with the exception of species that never have sex at all, such as sea urchins."

And same-sex love and attraction have clearly been around as long as we have, as evidenced in ancient art (including beautiful images of affectionate couples painted on Greek pottery thousands of years ago)

This group in San Francisco marched for marriage equality in California.

and literature. Anthropologists, who study human societies around the world, have found same-sex behavior in just about all of them.

The History of Homophobia

Prejudice against LGBT people, on the other hand, has not always existed—far from it. Among certain Native American tribes, "two-spirit people" (people who embodied both sexes) were highly respected as priests and healers. According to the research of Yale University historian John Boswell, ancient Christians had official rites for the blessing of gay marriages. And today, while homophobia rages in parts of the world where being gay is considered a serious crime punishable by death, in much of modern Western Europe, gay people enjoy full legal rights and acceptance as respected members of their communities.

But homophobia runs deep in Western culture and in the Judeo-Christian and Islamic religious traditions. In the ancient legal code of the Jewish people, preserved in the Book of Leviticus in the Jewish and Christian Bible, a man "lying" with another man was punishable by death. And in the 21st century, some Jews and Christians still point to these three-thousand-year-old tribal laws—supposedly dictated by God—to support their homophobia.

While ancient Rome was generally accepting of homosexuality, things changed under the influence of Christianity. The Emperor Constantius declared same-sex marriage illegal in the year 342, and the Christian emperors Valentian II, Theodosius I, and Arcadius declared homosexual sex to be illegal. Those who were found guilty of it were

This knight and his servant are being burned at the stake in medieval Switzerland for having a homosexual relationship.

condemned to be publicly burned alive. The emperor Justinian (526–575) claimed that homosexuals were responsible for famines and earthquakes, just as the Romans had blamed Christians for all kinds of troubles in earlier centuries.

For the next thousand-plus years, laws based on a particular inter-pretation of the Bible (and, as we explored in the previous chapter, a general "primitive brain" fear and distrust of people who are different) encouraged homophobia and hate crimes. While only enforced at certain times and in certain places, laws against homosexuality were enforced with jail sentences, public whippings, and even burning at the stake. Homosexuals were punished as criminals and sinners in old Europe in exactly the same way, and with the same Biblical authority, as were Jews and **heretics.** Meanwhile, great artists such as Leonardo Da Vinci and Michelangelo, men who were making enormous contributions to the art and culture of their era, may have been homosexual.

The early settlers of America brought their prejudices with them along with their other traditions. Strict laws against same-sex behavior, including the death penalty, were enacted in the Colonies. **Sodomy** laws, applying equally to gay and straight people but used almost exclu-sively against gays, still remained on the books in many U.S. states into the 21st century!

Homophobia in the Modern Era

With an increase in the understanding of scientific and psychological principles in the 1900s, what had been considered "sinful" behavior in the past began to be seen as normal human behavior for some people. Early sex researchers, such as Magnus Hirschfield (1868–1935) in Germany, argued that since homosexual behavior was just another human activity and did not hurt other people, it was simply not logical—and was, in fact, morally wrong—to punish it as a crime. Whether or not it was a "sin" was the problem of religious groups, Hirschfield believed, and should be completely separate from the concerns of government and law.

The **liberal** principles supported by the new science of psychology—as well as a call for the human rights of minorities—began to make

Almost all of these signs for an LGBT pride rally in Paris were vandalized. The sign reads, "This changes nothing for you, and it's important for us."

things easier for homosexuals, especially in Europe. But then the Nazis came to power in Germany in the 1930s, and that changed everything. Like Jews, gypsies, Communists, and other minorities, gay people were **persecuted** as "unfit to live" in Nazi-occupied Europe. Arrested and sent to concentration camps, thousands of gay people were executed or died from disease and starvation. They were forced to wear a pink triangle on their prison uniforms, which often set them apart for particularly brutal treatment.

 CLOSE-UP: NAZI PERSECUTION OF HOMOSEXUALS

These facts about the persecution of homosexuals by the Nazis from 1933 through 1945 come from the United States Holocaust Museum.

- Under Paragraph 175 of the criminal code, male homosexuality was illegal in Germany. The Nazis arrested an estimated 100,000 homosexual men, 50,000 of whom were imprisoned.

- During the Nazi regime, the police had the power to jail indefinitely—without trial—anyone they chose, including those deemed dangerous to Germany's moral fiber.

- Between 5,000 and 15,000 gay men were interned in concentration camps in Nazi Germany. These prisoners were marked by pink, triangular badges and, according to many survivor accounts, were among the most abused groups in the camps.

- Nazis interested in finding a "cure" for homosexuality conducted medical experiments on some gay concentration camp inmates. These experiments sometimes involved mutilation and caused illness and even death. They yielded no scientific knowledge.

And while American soldiers—quite a few of them LGBT—had fought bravely in World War II (1939–1945) for the principles of human liberation, they returned home to a country that was still racist, sexist, homophobic, and transphobic. In 1953 President Eisenhower signed Executive Order 10450, effectively barring LGBT people from government jobs under the guise of questioning loyalty and security risk from blackmail. (Parts of that Order remained in effect for 40 years until the 1990s and the Clinton administration). In the 1950s and '60s, men and women who gathered together in bars and clubs were subject to police raids, arrest, and public exposure. People's personal lives and careers were destroyed over something as simple as being caught dancing with a member of their own sex. Hate crimes against LGBT people—robbery, violence, and harassment—went unreported because of their fear of public exposure and rampant homophobia within law enforcement. Religious leaders preached against homosexual "sinners," families disowned and rejected their own LGBT sons and daughters, and LGBT people were oppressed and humiliated by laws that excluded and denied them their basic rights and protections as citizens. Most led lives of secrecy and denial in order to escape punishing social **stigma** and legal prosecution. The religious, legal, and medical establishments were united in their homophobia. In fact, homophobia was completely institutionalized in America—it was considered a legitimate way to feel.

It would take a strong and brave LGBT liberation movement, starting in the 1950s, to begin the long battle against this deeply ingrained homophobia.

After someone vandalized this car, the owner repainted it. Rather than simply painting over the graffiti, she used the word that had been scrawled across her car in a design to show that she is proud of who she is and refuses to hide her true self in fear.

TEXT-DEPENDENT QUESTIONS

- Is homosexual behavior exclusive to human beings?

- Have all human societies had a cultural aversion to homosexuality?

- How did early researchers in sex and psychology affect cultural views of homosexuality?

 RESEARCH PROJECTS

- Read the Bible's Book of Leviticus, and note the many other things that are forbidden besides same-sex behavior.

- Read some of Sigmund Freud's groundbreaking treatises on homosexuality.

- Investigate some of the movies, books, and plays on the subject of LGBT oppression during Germany's Third Reich.

A man reacts with tears of joy after hearing that the Supreme Court had upheld the rights of same-sex couples to marry in all states on June 26, 2015. The landmark U.S. Supreme Court ruling capped the biggest civil rights transformation in a half-century.

3

AN ONGOING STRUGGLE FOR RIGHTS AND RESPECT

 WORDS TO UNDERSTAND

Tolerance: Acceptance of, and respect for, other people's differences.

Internalized: Taken in; for example, when a person believes the negative opinions other people have of him, he has *internalized* their point of view and made it his own.

Empowering: Providing strength and energy; making someone feel powerful.

The struggle against homophobia is part of a larger movement toward human liberation that has been a major, positive theme in recent history. It has been a battle by minority groups for recognition by the majority, a call for equality under the law, and a reaction against the "primitive brain's" fear and hatred of "the Other" that has caused so much conflict and unhappiness in the history of the world. The battle has been fought in communities, in courts and legislatures around the world, and—just as important—in the hearts and minds of people. It is a continuing struggle of which we are all a part.

 CLOSE-UP: THE MATTHEW SHEPARD AND JAMES BYRD, JR. HATE CRIMES PREVENTION ACT

Congress passed the Matthew Shepard and James Byrd, Jr. Hate Crimes Prevention Act on October 22, 2009, and President Barack Obama signed it into law six days later. It was named after Matthew Shepard, who was murdered in an anti-gay hate crime in 1998 in Wyoming, and James Byrd, Jr., who was killed by white supremacists in an anti-black hate crime in the same year in Texas. The act expands the 1969 United States federal hate-crime law (which protected victims of hate crimes based on race or religion) to include crimes motivated by a victim's actual or perceived gender, sexual orientation, gender identity, or disability. The act gives federal authorities, such as the FBI, greater power to investigate hate crimes motivated by homophobia and trans-phobia, and it provides funding for state and local law enforcement to pursue and prosecute those who commit these crimes. The act is the first federal law to extend legal protections to LGBT victims of hate crimes, and it was supported by thirty-one state Attorneys General and more than 210 national law enforcement, professional, education, civil rights, religious, and civic organizations.

An Era of Change

The decade of the 1960s was a time of great social change in America and around the world. The Civil Rights movement, under the brilliant leadership of Dr. Martin Luther King, Jr., fought for the rights of African Americans who had suffered inequality, oppression, and segregation for over two centuries. By organizing, demonstrating, and standing up for themselves, African Americans made sure that their government and fellow citizens took their demands for full civil rights seriously. And they made tremendous political and social progress while teaching the world, in the phrase of the time, that "Black is Beautiful!"

Young people across America were opening their minds to new ideas. Hippies danced in the parks and called for peace and "flower power," college students protested an unpopular war in Vietnam, and many service members stationed in Vietnam seriously questioned what business their government had sending them there. It was an exciting time in America—an era of idealism, experimentation, and social change. Freedom was in the air. And the influence of both the African-American Civil Rights movement and the freedom-loving youth culture of the 1960s encouraged minority groups of all kinds to begin to freely express themselves in new ways. Movements for human liberation questioned the old assumptions of the establishment and called for a new society where difference and diversity would be celebrated, not feared. If black was beautiful, weren't brown and red and yellow beautiful, too? Didn't women deserve the same rights as men? Gay people, many of whom had been involved in the

This LGBT activist echoes the words of Martin Luther King Jr.'s "I Have a Dream" speech to call for LGBT rights and acceptance.

Nearly 50 years after the Stonewall Riots, the Stonewall Inn is still open for business. The sign reads, "Where Pride Began."

Civil Rights and youth culture movements, began to ask each other, "What about us?"

The Stonewall Riots

At 1:20 a.m. on June 28, 1969, police raided the Stonewall Inn in Greenwich Village, New York City. In 1969, it was illegal for people of the same sex to dance with each other in a public place, hold hands, or wear clothes that were not considered "normal" for their sex. Undercover police would come into gay bars and clubs and close them down. If the customers weren't lucky enough to slip out the back door, they were subject to arrest for "disorderly conduct" or "lewd behavior," and their names were listed in the newspaper. The typical New York gay bar was being raided once a month in the late 1960s, and the authorities were constantly bullying LGBT people.

But this night was different. Gathering on the street in front of the Stonewall, a group of angry people—among them transgender people, who had found themselves particular targets of the police—refused to be bullied. Fights broke out between the police and the crowd, windows were broken, parking meters smashed, and many arrests were made in what became known as "the Stonewall Riots."

Many historians consider the Stonewall Riots the beginning of the modern LGBT rights movement. Within days of the riots, a new political action group was formed in New York. Unlike earlier homosexual rights groups with vague-sounding names such as the Mattachine Society and Daughters of Bilitis, this one came right out and proudly called itself the Gay Liberation Front.

Gay Liberation and Gay Pride

The gay liberation movement, taking its cue from earlier equal-rights movements of the 1960s and 1970s, had three major goals: to encourage LGBT people to be proud of who they were, to demand full civil rights and equality under the law, and to educate the general public about gay people.

The political realm and the social world go hand-in-hand in all human liberation movements, and the fight for LGBT rights is no different. The battle against homophobia continues to be both political—working hard to make changes in the legal and governmental establishment—and social. Laws and institutions need to be changed, and the hearts and minds of people need to be won over to understanding, **tolerance**, and respect for diversity.

Men in New York City march for gay rights at the 1976 Democratic National Convention.

The 1970s was an exciting time for gay and lesbian people. Gay Pride was important to the developing LGBT communities in cities and towns across America. Gay people were encouraged to deal with the hurt of their own **internalized** homophobia and to express who they were proudly and openly to the world. This process was called "coming out of the closet" and meant the end to hiding in shame. Coming out was a brave and risky thing to do, especially in the early days of gay liberation.

Laws and institutions had not caught up with the social movement of "out-and-proud" LGBT people. Coming out could mean rejection from family and friends, the loss of a job, and an even greater chance of being a victim of homophobia and hate crimes.

But the openly gay pioneers made a tremendous difference in helping to change how the rest of the world saw gay people. Instead of living in the shadows like a scary, disliked "Other," LGBT people began coming out everywhere—in all their diversity. Not surprisingly, once they became visible, it turned out they weren't so different from everybody else! If every gay person came out, some people say, there would no longer be any such thing as homophobia. LGBT doctors, teachers, athletes, politicians, movie stars, aunts, uncles, parents, and friends would all come out to the world, and everyone would see that gay people are an important part of their lives, whether they realized it or not.

The AIDS Crisis

The AIDS crisis of the 1980s and '90s was both devastating and **empowering** to the gay community. Because AIDS was first identified

The AIDS Memorial Quilt, displayed here in Washington, D.C., is a powerful reminder of the AIDS epidemic and the lives it cut short. Each of the nearly 50,000 3-by-6-foot panels, sewn by friends, family, and lovers, commemorates the life of someone who died of AIDS.

as a "gay men's disease," a tremendous social stigma became attached to it. "Gay" began to equal "AIDS" in the minds of many, which meant that "gay" must be bad.

Some religious hate groups spread the idea that the disease was a judgment and punishment by an angry God against the homosexual lifestyle. Hate crimes increased on the streets of cities across America. Sick gay men were evicted from their apartments, rejected by their families, and refused medical treatment. Funding for AIDS research was delayed for years because the disease was seen as affecting groups of people that the majority didn't care much about, gay people, IV-drug users, and the poor.

Seeing no other choice, the gay community stepped up and organized to care for its own people. "AIDS buddies" cooked meals, walked dogs, and took AIDS patients to their medical appointments. The Gay Men's Health Crisis (GMHC) was founded by a group of gay doctors and community leaders in New York City in January of 1982; it was the world's first—and became the leading—provider of HIV/AIDS education, prevention, and care.

Frustrated and angered by the lack of government action in educating the general public about HIV/AIDS and in the funding of research and social programs, the AIDS Coalition to Unleash Power (ACT UP) was organized in 1987. The members of ACT UP were LGBT and proud and radical in their activities; they demanded that they be heard, that people with HIV/AIDS be taken seriously, and that LGBT people have the same rights as any other US citizen. They were committed to political action directed toward politicians and government agencies and to high-impact educational programs. More than twenty years later, they are still at it!

The New Millennium

The LGBT community entered the 21st century strong and proud. Gays and lesbians were finally being portrayed in movies and on television in more realistic ways, as more and more gay people came out and demanded to be recognized. Some people within the most powerful homophobic institutions, including the medical community and the church, committed themselves to reform their outdated prejudices. As early as 1972, the American Psychiatric Association declared that homosexuality was a normal human behavior and that gay people were not "sick." Since then, various religious denominations—including Reform Jews and Episcopalians—began working hard to make gay people feel welcome and empowered within their congregations.

In recent years, gay people and their allies have enjoyed victories in the courts at the state and federal levels that would have seemed impossible at the dawn of the gay liberation movement. Most recently, a huge milestone was achieved when marriage equality became the law of the land. In many ways, gay people have become **mainstream** in modern society.

But while acceptance of LGBT people and support for their rights continues to grow, the backlash from homophobic political and religious groups still gets in the way of progress and continues to influence public opinion. LGBT people are still the victims of violence and prejudice, and they still have a long way to go before they reach full equality politically and full acceptance in the hearts and minds of the majority.

U.S. President Barack Obama, right, looks to Judy and Dennis Shepard, parents of Matthew Shepard, during a reception at the White House to commemorate the signing of the Hate Crimes Prevention Act in Washington, D.C. on October 28, 2009. Matthew Shepard, who was gay, was killed in a hate crime in Laramie, Wyoming, in 1998.

TEXT-DEPENDENT QUESTIONS

- What are some of the social movements that helped influence gay liberation?
- Which group was the first to fight back at the Stonewall Riots?
- How did the AIDS epidemic change the gay rights movement?

 RESEARCH PROJECTS

- Find out more about the Stonewall Riots, ideally from first-hand accounts of its participants.
- Read some of the many AIDS memoirs that are available, with an eye toward learning how the epidemic both devastated and galvanized the community.

This student protesting Proposition 8, the California Marriage Protection Act, which denied same-sex couples the right to marry, is also protesting hatred in general.

I AM FIGHTING H8

4

WHAT CAN *YOU* DO ABOUT HOMOPHOBIA?

 WORDS TO UNDERSTAND

Victimized: Experienced unfair and negative treatment, like violence or bullying.
Offensive: Something that hurts other people's feelings, embarrasses them, or encourages negative stereotypes.

Young people, regardless of their sexual orientation, are growing up in a world where the full social acceptance of LGBT people is advancing with an energy never seen before in history. Opinion polls indicate that young people support such LGBT rights issues as marriage equality and adoption rights much more than their parents' and grandparents' generations do. And positive LGBT models are everywhere: in the sports and entertainment industry, in politics and religion, in your neighborhood, in your classroom, and in your family. Teenagers are coming out in large numbers, supported by Gay–Straight Alliances and anti-homophobia education programs in numerous schools. In many ways, this may be the best time ever to be an LGBT kid!

And yet, we know that middle schools and high schools are not easy places in which to be different. Peer pressure dominates the social world of adolescents. Teenagers have always split themselves into groups such as the popular kids, the jocks, the science nerds, and the partiers. A strong loyalty to your particular group is a big part of being a teenager. One group can decide it dislikes another group. Gossip can hurt people. And nothing hurts a young person more than rejection by peers. Where do LGBT kids (or those who might simply be questioning their sexual orientation) fit into your school and social worlds?

 CLOSE-UP: "THAT'S SO GAY!"

What's with kids using the word "gay" as an insult?

The use of "gay" as a negative adjective is an increasingly common practice in American culture. Many children and adults use the term to refer to anything bad, weak, or otherwise undesirable. Although kids may not have bad intentions when they say it, such language only reinforces the idea that "gay" = "bad." Also, the language can do significant damage to gay and lesbian students, who may feel they must endure it in silence in order to fit in.

(Adapted from nickelodeonparents.com)

These students are participating in the International Day of Silence, protesting how LGBT people have been harassed, abused, and silenced in schools.

Studies show that LGBT kids still have it rough. One study of 192 gay teenage boys found that one-third of them reported being verbally abused by one or more family members when they came out, and another 10 percent reported being physically assaulted. In a nationwide study of over 9,000 gay high school students, 24 percent of the boys reported being **victimized**, verbally or physically, at least *ten times* in the previous school year because of their sexual orientation; 11 percent of lesbians reported the same thing. Gay teenagers are four times more likely to be threatened with a deadly weapon than their straight peers. Teenage victims of homophobia often experience severe depression, a sense of helplessness, low self-esteem, and even suicidal thoughts (LGBT teenagers are almost five times more likely to attempt suicide than straight teenagers). And the negative family, school, and social pressures gay teenagers face can lead them to abuse drugs and alcohol, engage in unsafe sexual activity, and have body image and eating disorders.

Not a pretty picture, is it?

If you're a straight teenager, are you contributing to the unhappiness and insecurity—both physical and emotional—of gay and lesbian kids in your world?

Are You Homophobic?

Are YOU homophobic? Ask yourself:

- Do I have negative stereotypes of gay people?
- Do I participate in bullying or making fun of gay kids in my school, or allow it to happen even if I think it's wrong?
- Do I use hurtful language (like "fag" or "dyke") when talking about gay people? Do I use the word "gay" in a negative way, to mean something uncool ("That is so *gay!*")?
- Do I tell **offensive** jokes about gay and lesbian people? Or laugh at them?

- Do I *not* treat LGBT people with the same politeness and respect that I extend to other people?

If you answered "yes" to any of these questions, you may have to admit to yourself that you are homophobic. Think about whether you really want to be a part of that tired old system of racism, sexism, homophobia, and transphobia that has victimized innocent people and kept

The International Day Against Homophobia and Transphobia is held every year on May 17. The event provides an opportunity to celebrate diversity of all kinds and encourage respect for all people.

human beings apart for so long. It's the 21st century, and you are a global citizen of the future. Be proud of who you are, and support those who are different from you, so that they can feel proud, too—rather than hurt, scared, or depressed. Understanding, freedom, and love are what make life worth living for everyone. Maybe it is time to think about what side you want to be on!

If you're an LGBT teenager, take care of yourself physically and emotionally. Build yourself a support network. Concentrate on the people who love and appreciate you, and try not to worry about the people who don't understand how unique and wonderful you really are. There is no reason for you to feel alone or "abnormal" in a world where millions of LGBT people are living happy and proud lives, finding love, and doing good work in their communities. LGBT people have come a long way, thanks to the bravery and sacrifices of those who have gone before them. Be proud, be happy, and—together with your straight allies—fight homophobia!

TEXT-DEPENDENT QUESTIONS

- What kind of problems do LGBT teenagers face today?

- What kind of challenges does high school still present to LGBT students?

- What kind of pitfalls can LGBT students fall into, because of bullying and abuse?

 RESEARCH PROJECTS

- Find out whether your school has a Gay–Straight Alliance; if so, attend a meeting and see what issues it's dealing with.

- Examine your own mind and heart for fears and prejudices you might feel concerning LGBT people or other groups. If you find any, ask yourself where they might have come from and use the answer to help you move beyond them.

SERIES GLOSSARY

Activists: People committed to social change through political and personal action.

Advocacy: The process of supporting the rights of a group of people and speaking out on their behalf.

Alienation: A feeling of separation and distance from other people and from society.

Allies: People who support others in a cause.

Ambiguous: Something unclear or confusing.

Anonymous: Being unknown; having no one know who you are.

Assumption: A conclusion drawn without the benefit of real evidence.

Backlash: An adverse reaction by a large number of people, especially to a social or political development.

Bias: A tendency or preference toward a particular perspective or ideology that interferes with the ability to be impartial, unprejudiced, or objective.

Bigotry: Stubborn and complete intolerance of a religion, appearance, belief, or ethnic background that differs from one's own.

Binary: A system made up of two, and only two, parts.

Bohemian: Used to describe movements, people, or places characterized by nontraditional values and ways of life often coupled with an interest in the arts and political movements.

Caricature: An exaggerated representation of a person.

Celibate: Choosing not to have sex.

Chromosome: A microscopic thread of genes within a cell that carries all the information determining what a person is like, including his or her sex.

Cisgender: Someone who self-identifies with the gender he or she was assigned at birth.

Civil rights: The rights of a citizen to personal and political freedom under the law.

Clichés: Expressions that have become so overused—stereotypes, for example— that they tend to be used without thought.

Closeted: Choosing to conceal one's true sexual orientation or gender identity.

Compensating: Making up for something by trying harder or going further in the opposite direction.

Conservative: Cautious; resistant to change and new ideas.

Controversy: A disagreement, often involving a touchy subject about which differing opinions create tension and strong reactions.

Customs: Ideas and ways of doing things that are commonly understood and shared within a society.

Demonize: Portray something or someone as evil.

Denominations: Large groups of religious congregations united under a common faith and name, and organized under a single legal administration.

Derogatory: Critical or cruel, as in a term used to make a person feel devalued or humiliated.

Deviation: Something abnormal; something that has moved away from the standard.

Dichotomy: Division into two opposite and contradictory groups.

Discrimination: When someone is treated differently because of his or her race, sexual orientation, gender identity, religion, or some other factor.

Disproportionate: A situation where one particular group is overrepresented within a larger group.

Diverse: In the case of a community, one that is made up of people from many different backgrounds.

Effeminate: A word used to refer to men who have so-called feminine qualities.

Emasculated: Having had one's masculinity or manhood taken away.

Empathy: Feeling for another person; putting yourself mentally and emotionally in another person's place.

Empirical evidence: Factual data gathered from direct observation.

Empowering: Providing strength and energy; making someone feel powerful.

Endocrinologist: A medical doctor who specializes in the treatment of hormonal issues.

Epithets: Words or terms used in a derogatory way to put a person down.

The Establishment: The people who hold influence and power in society.

Extremist: Someone who is in favor of using extreme or radical measures, especially in politics and religion.

Flamboyant: Colorful and a bit outrageous.

Fundamentalist: Someone who believes in a particular religion's fundamental principles and follows them rigidly. When the word is used in connection with Christianity, it refers to a member of a form of Protestant Christianity that believes in the strict and literal interpretation of the Bible.

Gay liberation: The movement for the civil and legal rights of gay people that originated in the 1950s and emerged as a potent force for social and political change in the late 1960s and '70s.

Gender: A constructed sexual identity, whether masculine, feminine, or entirely different.

Gender identity: A person's self-image as female, male, or something entirely different, no matter what gender a person was assigned at birth.

Gender roles: Those activities and traits that are considered appropriate to males and females within a given culture.

Gene: A microscopic sequence of DNA located within a chromosome that determines a particular biological characteristic, such as eye color.

Genitalia: The scientific term for the male and female sex organs.

Genocide: The large-scale murder and destruction of a particular group of people.

Grassroots: At a local level; usually used in reference to political action that begins within a community rather than on a national or global scale.

Harassed/harassment: Being teased, bullied, or physically threatened.

Hate crime: An illegal act in which the victim is targeted because of his or her race, religion, sexual orientation, or gender identity.

Homoerotic: Having to do with homosexual, or same-sex, love and desire.

Homophobia: The fear and hatred of homosexuality. A homophobic person is sometimes referred to as a "homophobe."

Horizontal hostility: Negative feeling among people within the same minority group.

Hormones: Chemicals produced by the body that regulate biological functions, including male and female gender traits, such as beard growth and breast development.

Identity: The way a person, or a group of people, defines and understands who they are.

Inborn: Traits, whether visible or not, that are a part of who we are at birth.

Inclusive: Open to all ideas and points of view.

Inhibitions: Feelings of guilt and shame that keep us from doing things we might otherwise want to do.

Internalized: Taken in; for example, when a person believes the negative opinions other people have of him, he has *internalized* their point of view and made it his own.

Interpretation: A particular way of understanding something.

Intervention: An organized effort to help people by changing their attitudes or behavior.

Karma: The force, recognized by both Hindus and Buddhists, that emanates from one's actions in this life; the concept that the good and bad things one does determine where he or she will end up in the next life.

Legitimized: Being taken seriously and having the support of large numbers of people.

LGBT: An initialism that stands for lesbian, gay, bisexual, and transgender. Sometimes a "Q" is added (**LGBTQ**) to include "questioning." "Q" may also stand for "queer."

Liberal: Open to new ideas; progressive; accepting and supportive of the ideas or identity of others.

Liberation: The act of being set free from oppression and persecution.

Mainstream: Accepted, understood, and supported by the majority of people.

Malpractice: When a doctor or other professional gives bad advice or treatment, either out of ignorance or deliberately.

Marginalize: Push someone to the sidelines, away from the rest of the world.

Mentor: Someone who teaches and offers support to another, often younger, person.

Monogamous: Having only one sexual or romantic partner.

Oppress: Keep another person or group of people in an inferior position.

Ostracized: Excluded from the rest of a group.

Out: For an LGBT person, the state of being open with other people about his or her sexual orientation or gender identity.

Outed: Revealed or exposed as LGBT against one's will.

Persona: A character or personality chosen by a person to change the way others perceive them.

Pioneers: People who are the first to try new things and experiment with new ways of life.

Politicized: Aware of one's rights and willing to demand them through political action.

Prejudice: An opinion (usually unfavorable) of a person or a group of people not based on actual knowledge.

Proactive: Taking action taken in advance of an anticipated situation or difficulty.

Progressive: Supporting human freedom and progress.

Psychologists and psychiatrists: Professionals who study the human mind and human behavior. Psychiatrists are medical doctors who can prescribe pills, whereas clinical psychologists provide talk therapy.

Quackery: When an untrained person gives medical advice or treatment, pretending to be a doctor or other medical expert.

The Right: In politics and religion, the side that is generally against social change and new ideas; often used interchangeably with *conservative*.

Segregation: Historically, a system of laws and customs that limited African Americans' access to many businesses, public spaces, schools, and neighborhoods that were "white only."

Sexual orientation: A person's physical and emotional attraction to the opposite sex (heterosexuality), the same sex (homosexuality), both sexes (bisexuality), or neither (asexuality).

Sociologists: People who study the way groups of humans behave.

Spectrum: A wide range of variations.

Stereotype: A caricature; a way to judge someone, probably unfairly, based on opinions you may have about a particular group they belong to.

Stigma: A mark of shame.

Subculture: A smaller group of people with similar interests and lifestyles within a larger group.

Taboo: Something that is forbidden.

Theories: Ideas or explanations based on research, experimentation, and evidence.

Tolerance: Acceptance of, and respect for, other people's differences.

Transgender: People who identify with a gender different from the one they were assigned at birth.

Transphobia: Fear or hatred of transgender people.

Variance: A range of differences within a category such as gender.

Victimized: Subjected to unfair and negative treatment, including violence, bullying, harassment, or prejudice.

FURTHER RESOURCES

The Matthew Shepard Foundation Website
Home page of the nonprofit LGBT support organization.
www.matthewshepard.org

The Concept of "the Other"
An examination of what otherness means in both theory and practice.
academic.brooklyn.cuny.edu/english/melani/cs6/other.html

Homophobia, HIV, and AIDS
How fear of LGBT intersects with the stigma of the virus.
www.avert.org/homophobia-hiv-and-aids.htm

Nazi Persecution of Homosexuality
An essay from the United States Holocaust Memorial Museum website.
www.ushmm.org/information/exhibitions/online-features/special-focus/nazi-persecution-of-homosexuals

The Two Spirit Tradition in Native American Experience
An examination of same-sex love that thrived in certain tribes.
www.gay-art-history.org/gay-history/gay-customs/native-american-homosexuality/two-spirit-native-american-gay.html

LGBT Rights by Country or Territory
Maps and texts showing the distribution of rights across the globe.
en.wikipedia.org/wiki/LGBT_rights_by_country_or_territory

Homophobia
An explanation and examination of how homophobia works in our world.
www.adl.org/hate-patrol/homophobia.asp

GLSEN (the Gay, Lesbian & Straight Education Network)
GLSEN is the leading national education organization focused on ensuring safe and affirming schools for all students. GLSEN seeks to develop school climates where difference is valued for the positive contribution it makes to creating a more vibrant and diverse community.
www.glsen.org

The Gay-Straight Alliance Network
Home page of the organization that works to make safer schools and reduce bullying.
www.gsanetwork.org

INDEX